MY FIRST BOOK

PERU

ALL ABOUT PERU FOR KIDS

GL⦿BED
CHILDREN BOOKS

Interior and cover Design: Daniel Day
Editor: Margaret Bam

For My Sons, Daniel, David and Jude

Cercado de Lima, Perú

Peru

Peru is a **country**.

A country is land that is controlled by a **single government**. Countries are also called **nations, states, or nation-states**.

Countries can be **different sizes**. Some countries are big and others are small.

Cusco, Peru

Where Is Peru?

Peru is located in the continent of South America.

A continent is a massive area of land that is separated from others by water or other natural features.

Peru is situated in the western part of South America.

Historic Center, Lima, Peru

Capital

The capital of Peru is Lima.

Lima is located in the **central west region** of the country.

Lima is the largest city in Peru.

Fabric store in Peru

Regions

Peru is a country that is made up of 25 regions

The regions of Peru are as follows:

Amazonas, Ancash, Apurimac, Arequipa, Ayacucho, Cajamarca, Callao, Cusco, Huancavelica, Huanuco, Ica, Junín, La Libertad, Lambayeque, Lima, Loreto, Madre de Dios, Moquegua, Pasco, Piura, Puno, San Martín, Tacna, Tumbes, Ucayali.

Cusco, Peru

Population

Peru has population of around **34 million people** making it the 45th most populated country in the world and the 4th most populated country in South America.

The majority of Peru's population lives in its urban areas, particularly in the coastal region where the cities of Lima, Arequipa, and Trujillo are located.

Miraflores, Lima, Peru

Size

Peru is **1,285,216 square kilometres** making it the third-largest country in South America and the 19th largest country in the world.

Peru is bordered by five countries: Ecuador to the north, Colombia to the northeast, Brazil to the east, Bolivia to the southeast, and Chile to the south.

Languages

The official language of Peru is **Spanish**, which was introduced by Spanish colonizers in the 16th century. However, Peru is also home to many indigenous languages, such as Quechua and Aymara, which have been spoken in the region for thousands of years.

Here are a few Spanish phrases
- **¿Cómo estás?**- How are you?
- **Mucho gusto** - Nice to meet you
- **De nada** - You're welcome

Machu Picchu

Attractions

There are lots of interesting places to see in Peru.

Some beautiful places to visit in Peru are

- Machu Picchu
- Colca Canyon
- Saqsaywaman
- Nazca Lines
- Sacred Valley
- Lima Main Square

Puno, Peru

History of Peru

Peru has a rich history that dates back over 10,000 years. It was home to many indigenous cultures, including the Inca Empire, which ruled over much of South America until the arrival of the Spanish in the 16th century.

The Spanish conquest of Peru which began on 16 November 1532 was one of the most important campaigns in the Spanish colonization of the Americas.

Peru gained independence from Spain on 28 July 1821.

Lake Titicaca, Peru

Customs in Peru

Peru has a rich cultural heritage with many customs and traditions that have been passed down through generations.

- Peru is known for its lively and colourful festivals and celebrations such as Inti Raymi, Día de los Muertos and Carnaval.
- Peru has a long tradition of textile weaving, dating back to pre-Columbian times. Many indigenous communities still produce textiles using traditional techniques, and these textiles are highly valued for their quality and beauty.

Music of Peru

Peru has a rich musical tradition that blends indigenous, African, and European influences. Some popular music genres in Peru include Andean music, Huayno, Afro-Peruvian music, Música criolla and Peruvian cumbia.

Some notable Peruvian musicians include
- A.CHAL - A Peruvian-American singer-songwriter, rapper, and record producer.
- Renata Flores - a Peruvian singer, made famous in South America by a viral Quechua cover of Michael Jackson's "The Way You Make Me Feel".

Fish ceviche

Food of Peru

Peru is known for having delicious, flavoursome and rich dishes.

The national dish of Peru is **Ceviche** which is a delicious fresh raw fish salad marinated in lime with salt and mixed with onion, garlic, and other peppers.

Lomo saltado

Food of Peru

Peruvian cuisine is known for its diverse flavors and ingredients, which reflect the country's multicultural heritage.

Some popular dishes in Peru include

- **Lomo saltado: A stir-fry dish that combines beef, onions, tomatoes, and French fries. It is typically served with rice.**
- **Causa: A layered dish made with mashed potatoes, avocado, and seafood. It is typically garnished with boiled eggs and olives.**

Vale Sagrado, Cusco, Peru

Weather in Peru

Peru is a big country and its weather varies considerably from north to south. The northern region has an equatorial climate with hot and humid weather all year round and frequent rainfall, while in the southern region the climate is tropical.

Lama in Macchu Picchu, Peru

Animals of Peru

There are many wonderful animals in Peru.

Here are some animals that live in Peru

- Jaguar
- Hummingbirds
- Blue Morpho Butterfly
- Andean Cock-of-the-Rock
- Alpacas
- Llamas

Sports of Peru

Sports play an integral part in Peruvian culture. The most popular sport is **Football.**

Here are some of famous sportspeople from Peru

- **Teófilo Cubillas - Football**
- **Sofia Mulanovich - Surfing**
- **Luis Horna - Tennis**
- **Alejandro Olmedo - Tennis**
- **Natalia Málaga - Volleyball**

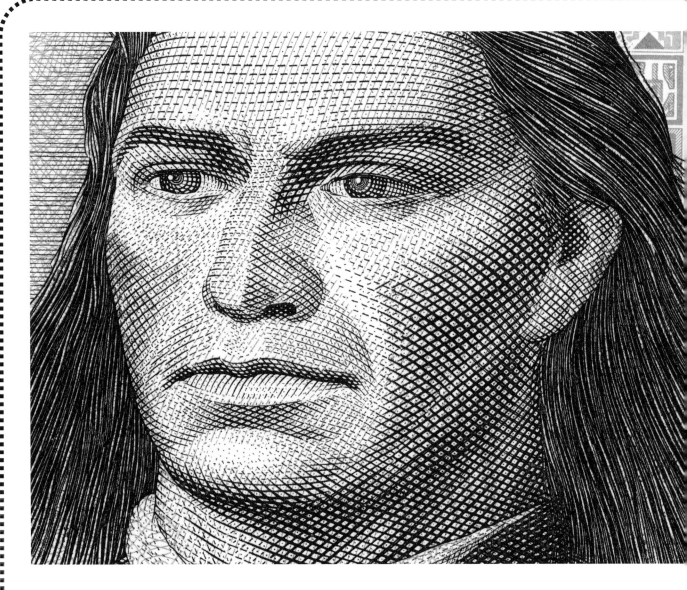

Tupac Amaru II

Famous

Peru has produced many notable figures in various fields, including politics, literature, music, sports, and science.

Here are some notable Peruvian figures

- **César Vallejo – Poet**
- **Henry Ian Cusick – Actor**
- **Claudio Pizarro – Football**
- **Paolo Guerrero – Football**
- **Alejandro Toledo – Politician**
- **Tupac Amaru II - Cacique**

Lima, Peru

Something Extra...

As a little something extra, we are going to share some lesser known facts about Peru.

- **Peru is known for its wide variety of potatoes, with over 3,000 different types of potatoes grown in the country.**
- **Peru is also home to Lake Titicaca, the highest navigable lake in the world.**
- **The beloved character Paddington Bear was inspired by a real-life bear from Peru.**

Words From the Author

We hope that you enjoyed learning about the wonderful country of Peru.

Peru is a country rich in culture and beauty, with lots of wonderful places to visit and people to meet.

We hope you continue to learn more about this wonderful nation. If you enjoyed this book, consider leaving a review!

With Love